Baby Owl's Rescue

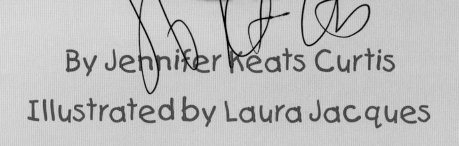

By Jennifer Keats Curtis

Illustrated by Laura Jacques

One warm April evening, Maddie grabbed a bat, a ball, and two mitts and ventured into the yard to practice catching pop-ups with her little brother, Max. As they trotted toward the back fence, Maddie heard a funny noise.

Clack, clack, clack.

What was it? It sounded like fingernails tapping on a table top.

Clack, clack, clack.

There it was again. Maddie was sure it was coming from beneath the pine tree in the far corner of the yard. She flung down her mitt, put a finger to her lips, and shushed Max.

As she crept closer, she saw something gray and fuzzy. Were those feathers?

Yes! Huge, bright yellow eyes peered up at her from inside a feathery, ruffled, little ball. Maddie could see a sharp beak, furry feet, and big, long talons.

Clack, clack, clack, continued the baby owl, clapping its pointed bill quickly, warning Maddie to go away!

Even though the baby owl was cute and cuddly, Maddie and Max knew that it was important not to treat a wild animal as a pet. Fortunately for Maddie and Max, their mother was a wildlife rehabilitator, trained to care for injured, wild animals.

The children knew that a baby bird on the ground might not need human help. Its parents were probably nearby. Wanting to do what was best for the baby owl, they ran to get their mother.

As soon as their mother saw the yellow eyes, she knew what type of owl the children had found. She pointed to the feathery horns beginning to grow. "It's a Great Horned Owl!" she whispered excitedly.

She reminded her kids that they had heard a pair of Great Horned Owls calling to each other after the New Year. Great Horned Owls nest earlier than other birds, often laying their eggs as early as January, even with snow on the ground.

Throughout the long, cold winter, the whole family had heard the *whoo-hoo-ho-o-o* as the parents softly called to each other. Then, once the babies hatched, the parents became silent.

"How old is he, Mom?" Max whispered.

"I think he's a brancher; he is just leaving the nest."

"Why is he on the ground?" asked Maddie.

"What should we do?" Max asked worriedly.

Their mother smiled and silently pointed up. Near the top of a very tall tree, the kids could just make out a nest of messy sticks. "He was either blown out of his nest by those strong winds last night, or he fell as he was hopping from branch to branch. Let's see if he's old enough to climb back into the nest himself."

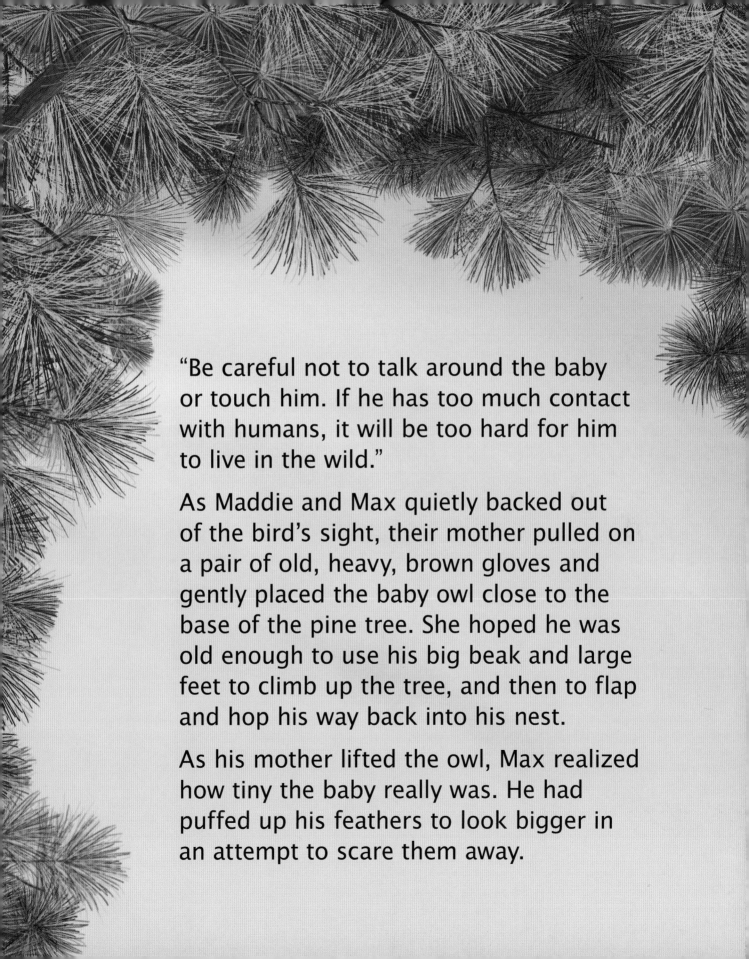

"Be careful not to talk around the baby or touch him. If he has too much contact with humans, it will be too hard for him to live in the wild."

As Maddie and Max quietly backed out of the bird's sight, their mother pulled on a pair of old, heavy, brown gloves and gently placed the baby owl close to the base of the pine tree. She hoped he was old enough to use his big beak and large feet to climb up the tree, and then to flap and hop his way back into his nest.

As his mother lifted the owl, Max realized how tiny the baby really was. He had puffed up his feathers to look bigger in an attempt to scare them away.

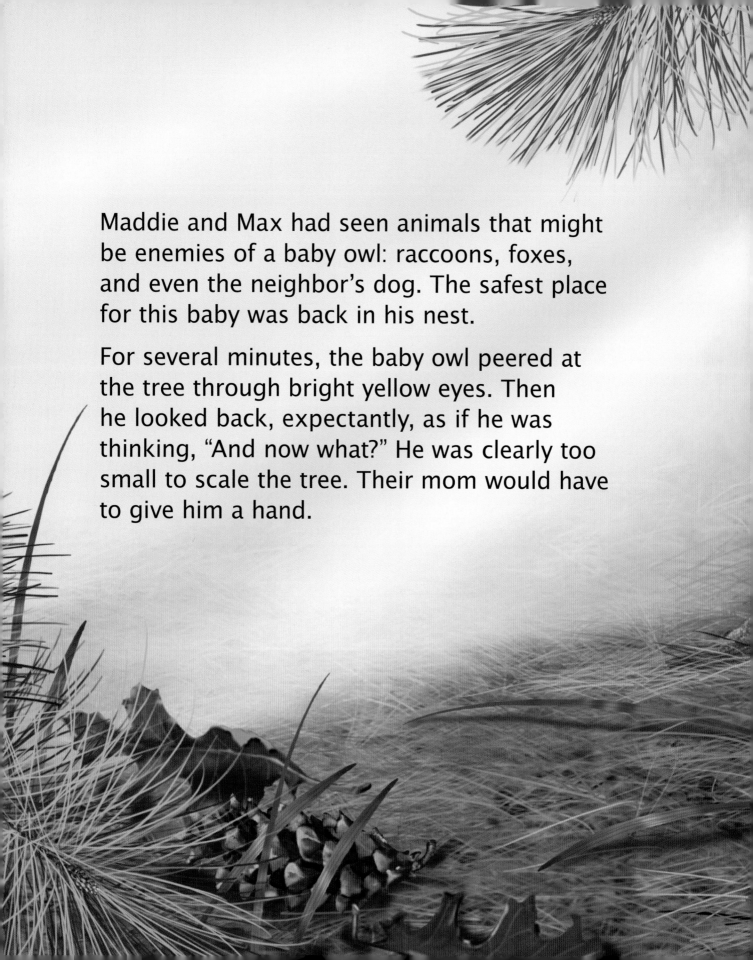

Maddie and Max had seen animals that might be enemies of a baby owl: raccoons, foxes, and even the neighbor's dog. The safest place for this baby was back in his nest.

For several minutes, the baby owl peered at the tree through bright yellow eyes. Then he looked back, expectantly, as if he was thinking, "And now what?" He was clearly too small to scale the tree. Their mom would have to give him a hand.

Grinning, their mother asked her children to make sure no other animals came near the baby owl as she ran into the house. A moment later, she returned with a laundry basket. She intended to make the baby a new nest!

Maddie and Max helped their mother fill the basket with small branches.

Maddie and Max had seen their mother make a phone call but were surprised when two firefighters arrived in a shiny red and white "cherry picker" truck. As they, and several neighbors, watched, one of the firefighters put on a helmet and climbed into the cherry picker basket.

Using her heavy gloves, their mother placed the owl in the basket nest and then handed it to the firefighter. He rose high in the air until he was several feet under the nest from which the baby had fallen. He carefully placed the basket in the crook of the tree and tied it just below the old nest.

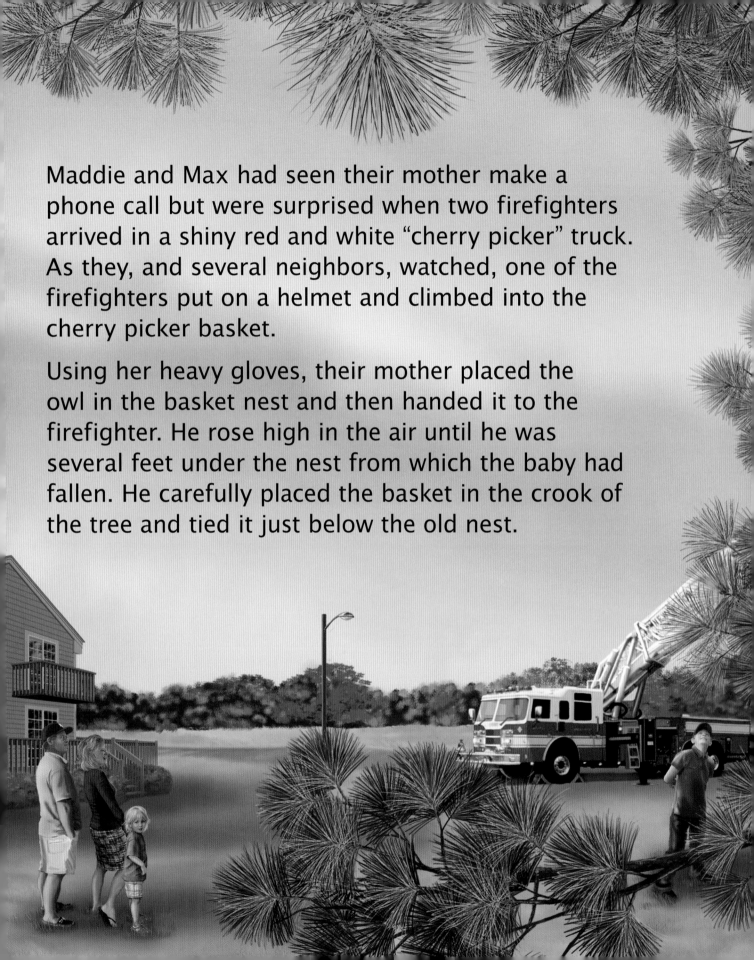

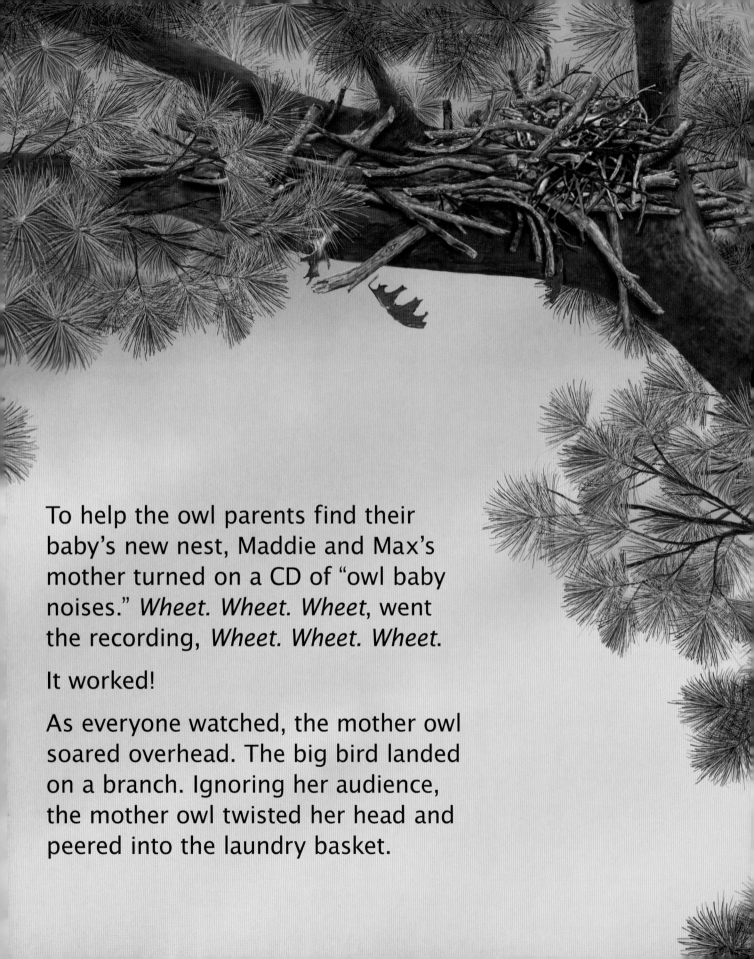

To help the owl parents find their baby's new nest, Maddie and Max's mother turned on a CD of "owl baby noises." *Wheet. Wheet. Wheet*, went the recording, *Wheet. Wheet. Wheet.*

It worked!

As everyone watched, the mother owl soared overhead. The big bird landed on a branch. Ignoring her audience, the mother owl twisted her head and peered into the laundry basket.

Powerfully, the mother owl swooped off
again, in search of a mouse, a gopher, or
lizard, to feed her hungry baby.

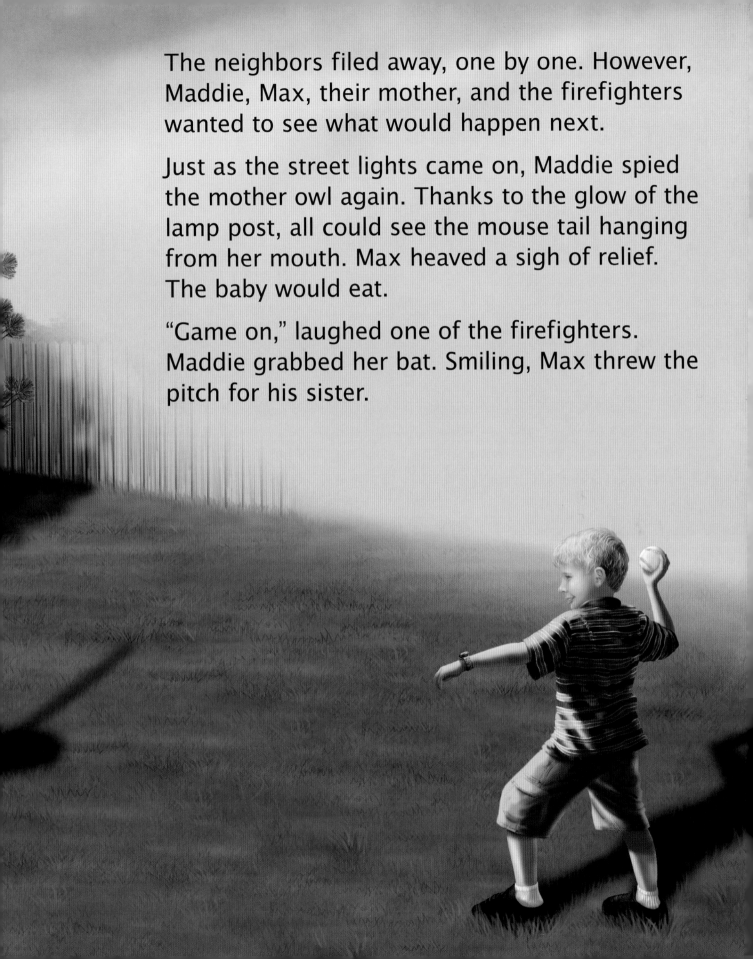

The neighbors filed away, one by one. However, Maddie, Max, their mother, and the firefighters wanted to see what would happen next.

Just as the street lights came on, Maddie spied the mother owl again. Thanks to the glow of the lamp post, all could see the mouse tail hanging from her mouth. Max heaved a sigh of relief. The baby would eat.

"Game on," laughed one of the firefighters. Maddie grabbed her bat. Smiling, Max threw the pitch for his sister.

For Creative Minds

Great Horned Owl Fun Facts

They weigh between 3 and 4 lbs. (1.36-1.81 kg.). Find something that weighs about the same to compare.

Like other owls, they are nocturnal. That means they hunt at night and sleep during the day.

Adults are between 18 and 25 inches or 46 to 63 centimeters.

We think they can live to be about 12 or 13 years old in the wild. Their main predators are other Great Horned Owls.

Great Horned Owls are found in all kinds of habitats: in your backyard, deserts, forests, and even in the Arctic!

A few hours after eating, they throw up pellets of fur, feathers, bones, and other undigested parts of their meals. These pellets help us to understand what owls eat.

Females are a little larger than the males.

The loud *hoo-hoo hoooooo hoo-hoo* can be heard for miles during a still night but they will not call while hunting. They don't want to let their prey know where they are.

They are birds of prey. Their food is alive when they catch it. They eat mice, squirrels, rabbits, skunks, crows, herons, other owls, ducks, frogs, some fish, and even some domestic cats. They swallow small prey whole, but will tear larger animals apart using their talons and beaks.

When flying, their wingspan (measured from the tip of one wing to the tip of the other wing), can be approximately twice their size. Hold out your arms and have someone measure your "armspan." How does it compare to an owl's wingspan?

Great Horned Owl Adaptation Matching Activity

A.

1. Large, yellow eyes help them to see at night.

2. Sharp beaks help them tear larger prey to eat.

B.

3. The front edge of each wing has comb-like bristles to muffle the wing's flapping noise. This helps owls to silently sneak up on prey.

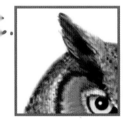

C.

4. Like most birds, owls have four toes. But one of the toes can swivel forward or backwards so that it can hold onto things with three toes in front, one in back or two facing frontward and backward!

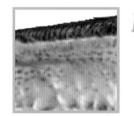

D.

5. Sharp, curved talons (claws) are used to grab prey.

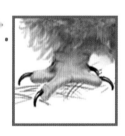

E.

6. The brown, gray colors and designs in the feathers help owls to blend, or to camouflage, themselves into trees.

7. They can't move their eyes but they can turn their heads almost all the way around (270 degrees) to see.

F.

G.

8. Their ears are holes on the side of their heads, right behind their eyes. The ears are off-centered; one is a little higher than the other. The difference in ear height helps the owls to judge the distance of sound. The feather tufts or "horns" are simple decorations to make the birds more fierce looking.

H.

Answers: 1G, 2F, 3D, 4E, 5A, 6H, 7B, 8C

Owl Life Cycle Sequencing Activity

If desired, copy or download the cards, cut out, and put in numerical order for the correct sequence of events.

1 In January or February, the male and female will call to each other as part of their "dating" or courtship.

2 An owl pair will take over other birds' nests. They are not picky about where the nest is and will use a nest in trees, on the side of cliffs, or even on buildings.

3 The female usually lays two or three white eggs at a time.

4 Both parents incubate the eggs for 26 to 35 days (about a month, give or take). They will guard the nest and will either kill or drive off any other animal that tries to get to it.

5 When born, the hatchlings are covered with a white down.

6 When they are about 6 or 7 weeks old, young start to walk around on branches near the nest. They are called branchers, like the owl in the story.

7 Both parents continue to feed their young until the young leave the nest and fly off to find their own home. This happens the fall after they are born.

8 The young owls can fly when they are about 9 or 10 weeks old and are then called fledglings.

What to Do if You Find an Injured Bird

Even if you find a baby bird on the ground, it may not need your help.

Most of the time, chicks are being watched by their parents and do not need your help.

Unless you can see that the bird is hurt, or it has been alone for many hours, leave it where it is. Keep your pets away (by keeping them in the house or on a leash) so that the bird's parents will feed it.

While it is not true that a mother bird will abandon her baby if she smells a human scent, you should not handle the baby unless you are able to put it back in its nest. Most birds do not have a good sense of smell (except vultures). It is your presence, not your scent, that might keep them from coming back for the baby. It is best to keep human activity at a minimum around the chick or the nest, if possible. If you must pick it up, wear gloves and wash your hands afterwards.

If you believe that the baby has been orphaned or is hurt, please contact your state's Department of Natural Resources or veterinarian to find a licensed rehabilitator near you. Rehabilitators, often called rehabbers, have special permits and training that allow them to take care of animals that are hurt, sick, or orphaned. Rehabbers care for wildlife, sometimes in a home or clinic, but they work to help the animals remain in nature. They release these creatures as soon as they can fend for themselves.

Until you can get the bird to a rehabber, keep it in a small box, lined with a clean, soft cloth in a quiet, dark area. Do not give the baby anything to eat or drink.

It is illegal to possess or capture owls and migratory birds in any state if you are not licensed to do so.

For my parents, Bea and Neil Keats, who taught me compassion, and my brother, Matt, who tested its limits. With love, — JKC

To my parents Bob and Lil Yaglowski, who always make sure that ALL of their owlets are safely tucked into their nests at night. With love, respect and sheer admiration, — LJ

To help Kathy Woods continue her work rehabilitating wild animals, the author donates a portion of the royalties from sales of this book to the Phoenix Wildlife Center.

Thanks to Kathleen Woods, Wildlife Rehabilitator/Director of the Phoenix Wildlife Center, Inc; Ken Lockwood, Program Director at the Eagle Valley Raptor Center; Jim Fitzpatrick, Executive Director, Carpenter St. Croix Valley Nature Center; and Rob Fergus, Senior Scientist, Urban Bird Conservation, National Audubon Society, for verifying the accuracy of the information in this book.

Publisher's Cataloging-In-Publication Data

Curtis, Jennifer Keats.

  Baby owl's rescue / by Jennifer Keats Curtis ; illustrated by Laura Jacques.

  p. : col. ill. ; cm.

  Summary: What if you found a baby owl in your backyard? Would you know what to do? Where would you go to find help? Join young Maddie and Max as they learn a valuable lesson. Includes "For Creative Minds" section.

ISBN: 978-1-934359-95-2 (hardcover)
ISBN: 978-1-607180-40-1 (pbk.)
ISBN: 978-1-607180-60-9 (English eBook)
ISBN: 978-1-607180-50-0 (Spanish eBook)

1. Wildlife rescue--Juvenile literature. 2. Owls--Juvenile literature.
3. Wildlife rescue. 4. Owls. I. Jacques, Laura. II. Title.

QL83.2 .C87 2009
639.9   2009926404

Lexile Level 900; Lexile Code AD

Manufactured in China, January, 2011 This product conforms to CPSIA 2008
2 3 4 5 6 7 8 9 10

Sylvan Dell Publishing
976 Houston Northcutt Blvd., Suite 3
Mt. Pleasant, SC 29464